Our Lonely Journey

Remembering The Kindertransports

Our Lonely Journey

Remembering The Kindertransports

Stephen D. Smith
with
Steven Mendelsson, Vera Schaufeld and Lisa Vincent
with Illustrations by Hans Jackson

Our Lonely Journey
Remembering The Kindertransports

Published in Great Britain by
Quill Press, The Holocaust Centre
The Hub
Haskell House
152 West End Lane
London
NW6 1SD

First published in 1999 by
Paintbrush Publications

Text © 1999 Stephen D. Smith
Illustrations © 1999 Hans Jackson

British Library Catalogue in Publication Data
A catalogue record for this book is available from the British Library

ISBN 0-9536280-0-1

All rights reserved. No part of this publication may be reproduced in any form or by any means, electronic, mechanical, photocopying, recording or otherwise, without the prior permission of the publisher.

Design and Artwork, The National Holocaust Centre and Museum
Printed in England by Jellyfish Print Solutions, Swanmore

Photograph Acknowledgments
Quill Press would like to thank the following for allowing their photographs to be reproduced in this book: The Holocaust Centre, 1, 2, 8, 22; David Gordon, Topham Picturepoint, 5; Yad Vashem, 6; Main Commission for the investigation of Nazi War Crimes, courtesy of USHMM Photo Archives, 13; Wiener Library, 11; and Steven Mendelsson, Vera Schaufeld and Lisa Vincent, for the use of their personal collections.

Remembering

Steven Mendelsson, Lisa Vincent and Vera Schaufeld are all over 65 years old. When they were much younger, they experienced things that they would never wish their children or grandchildren to see or experience again. They are different people who were born in different cities and today live very different lives, but there are two things which they share in common. They are all Jewish and they all arrived in this country as children who had been sent here by their parents to help them escape from Hitler and the Nazis.

In this book, you will learn a little about their lives and what happened when the Nazis came to power in Germany. You will also find out how they were able to come to England with 10,000 other children on special trains called the *Kindertransports*, or Children's Transports.

When we remember things that happened in the past, we learn about each other. We can also learn a lot from each other. One beautiful sunny day in June 1999, 60 years after their arrival in England, Lisa, Steven and Vera met each other for the first time. In this book, you can read what they said to each other. Their stories are similar but not the same, because no two people have exactly the same story to tell.

1

Before they begin their conversation together, they would like to introduce themselves to you...

Steven Mendelsson: "I was born in Breslau in 1926. My grandfather, Samuel, started a very successful transport firm. My father enjoyed photography and my mother was very keen on physical fitness. I have a brother, Walter, four years younger than me. Breslau was in Germany then, but today it is the city of Wroclaw in Poland. I came to England on the Children's Transport in April 1939 to escape the Nazis. Today, I am married to Hillary and have three grown-up children of my own."

Vera Schaufeld: "I was born in 1930 in Prague, Czechoslovakia. My mother was German, but finished her studies in Prague after she met my father. They lived in his home town of Klatovy. He was a leader in the Jewish community, but also very proud to be Czech. The Nazis invaded Czechoslovakia in March 1939, a few months before the Second World War began, and my parents decided to send me to England for safety. I came on the *Kindertransport* in June 1939 and now live in London with my husband. I have two daughters and four grandchildren."

Lisa Vincent: "I was born in Nuremberg in 1923, which makes me the oldest of the three of us! My grandparents had the biggest toy factory in the world. I had so many toys I did not have time to enjoy them all properly. My mother was German and Jewish; my father was a German Catholic. I grew up partly as a Christian, but I was aware that my mother's family was Jewish and we went to synagogue from time to time. I have two older brothers. Today I live alone, but I have a daughter and two grandchildren of whom I am very proud. I left Germany on the last *Kindertransport* in August 1939.

Life before Hitler

Lisa before the war

"When I was still in primary school, my parents moved to a little village outside the city of Nuremberg," said Lisa. "It was a lovely little rural village, and what I remember most is the cherry blossom. I can remember sitting on the wall, watching people come out of the city on a Sunday, with cherry blossom trees right down the street."

"For me, the fondest memory is just a happy childhood," replied Vera, "the memory of being loved. I was an only child and I think I felt that I was cared for in my family. I particularly enjoyed it when aunts and uncles visited and I had the feeling of family around me. Later, I had no family, and maybe that is why those memories have become so important to me."

"I remember growing up in very nice surroundings," said Steven. "We had lots of friends where we lived in the suburbs of the city. We did not have a very religious home, but I remember a very large synagogue where I was taken on the special Jewish holidays, such as Rosh Hashanah, the Jewish New Year. There was space for about 3,000 people in the synagogue, so you can imagine what it was like on such days."

"Our home was not very religious either, that is until my grandmother came to live with us," Vera said, laughing a little.

"Yes, it's always the grandmothers who remind you who you are," smiled Lisa.

Vera with her grandmother

"After Grandmother arrived, we started to keep kosher, that is the special set of Jewish rules about food," Vera continued. "Before that, my parents were not too worried about Jewish practices. I went to the primary school nearby and had lots of friends. A couple of them were Jewish; the rest were not. I knew that I was Jewish, but it was not very important in our lives."

"I think we were proud to be German," said Lisa, holding her head high. "It was a way of feeling a part of everything. So being Jewish came second to being German."

"Yes. My grandfather was proud that he had done so much for the city and was so happy with all the honours bestowed upon him. He did not believe Hitler would do anything to him. Sadly, he was wrong," said Steven.

Steven's family

"My father was the same about Czechoslovakia," said Vera. "He felt very strongly that it was a wonderful country and that nothing would ever go wrong there. He had no idea at the time that one day the Nazis would take Czechoslovakia and that everything would change so much."

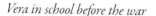

Vera in school before the war

How things changed

"From what I can remember, things did not change quickly when the Nazis came to power in Germany," said Steven. "I went to school as before. But then after a while, I had to go to the Jewish school. What I do remember is coming out of school and finding young boys in Hitler Youth uniforms, ready to beat us up. Often there would be three or four boys from the Hitler Youth against one Jewish student. Frequently, I would arrive home with my nose bleeding, with scratches on my knees and bruises on my arms. This would happen three or four times each week."

Hatred of Jews taught in class

"Because one of my parents was German, I did not have to go to the Jewish school to begin with," said Lisa, "but I do remember that there were a few Jewish girls in my school who left the country. In 1935, Hitler started new laws that meant Jews could no longer be citizens of Germany. They were not allowed to marry German people either. My father left my mother and took my two brothers to South America. Mother and I stayed in our house for a short while, but we were soon told to leave the village."

"Quite a lot of people who had been friendly suddenly ignored you," remembered Steven.

"Yes, I remember when one of our neighbours came and wished my mother goodbye in the street because she was not going to talk to her again," said Lisa.

"But I was most upset not to be able to join in with my friends. I could not go on school trips or go swimming, or even wear the same clothes. When the girls came in wearing brown Nazi bomber jackets I had a similar one made, but mine was blue and didn't have a swastika on it."

"It was different for me because I was younger and the Nazis only arrived in Czechoslovakia six years after they began ruling Germany," said Vera. "I was very aware of the day the Nazis marched in. Everyone was standing around listening to the radio. It was extremely tense and people were frightened about what would happen. I remember my nurse was very upset because she said that the British had let us down, as they should have helped us more.

Hitler talking to crowds

"On the first day, my father was arrested and taken away and I was not allowed to go to school. A few days later, my father came home and I went back to school again. My teacher, whom I had really liked, said that the Jews would be the first to run away from the Nazis, which was not true. I felt terribly upset. Suddenly I felt I was different."

She paused. "I also remember our radio being taken from us. Only my grandmother and I were in the house when the German soldiers banged on the door. I was really frightened. But they had only come for our radio."

"Our jewellery was taken in the same way," said Lisa. "They took our jewellery and then collected all the family silver and loaded it onto a lorry."

Hitler Youth on parade

What our parents said

Lisa's grandparents

"In 1938, the Nazis started to make life very frightening," said Lisa. "I remember the night they now call 'The Night of Broken Glass,' or *Kristallnacht* in German. During the night of 9 November, my mother and I were dragged from our flat and had to stand in our nightgowns in the town square. The Nazis were taking the men away, smashing windows and destroying homes. We had a beautiful grand piano and they just axed it straight in half. The smell of burning was everywhere."

"Yes, I remember that day, too," said Steven. "We were warned by neighbours not to go to school and later in the evening, the Nazis set the synagogue on fire. During the night, they came to find my father and grandfather. The caretaker of our building risked his life and told the Nazis they were too late, and that my father and grandfather had been collected ten minutes earlier. Four days later, when my father thought it was safe to return to work, he left the house in the morning as usual. That night he did not come back. He had been sent to a concentration camp."

"Did he survive?" asked Vera.

"Yes, he did. He was released in January, because he had fought for Germany in the First World War, but he had been beaten and was in a very bad way. He was too ill to see us children for several weeks."

"I seem to remember it was after *Kristallnacht* that the British Government offered a chance for Jewish children in Germany to come to England," said Lisa.

"They called the trains that were organised *Kindertransports*, that is, Children's Transports, because they were full of children leaving without their parents. Until this time, my mother had not said much about the Nazis. I was just told to be quiet, not to laugh too loud or to shout in the street, to blend into the background."

"My parents did not discuss things with me either, but we all knew what was happening," said Steven. "We had seen it. My father had experienced it. We knew what the Nazis were about and we just wanted to leave Germany."

"I had an aunt and uncle living in Germany," remembered Vera, "but I think my parents didn't want me to know what was going on. One day after school, my mother came to fetch me, which was unusual as I usually walked home with my friends. She took me to a nearby park and we sat on a bench together. She told me that she and my father had decided to send me to England. Then, two weeks later, she told me that because my father and grandmother were not able to come too, I was to travel alone and they would come as quickly as they could. She told me that they were going to write to me in a secret code, and from the code I would be able to know if they were alright and how soon they would be able to come. And so I got ready to leave."

Steven's parents,
Franz and Margarete

Time to say goodbye

"Did your parents have to make a list of what you had to take on the *Kindertransport* and show it to the Nazis?" asked Lisa.

"No. In Czechoslovakia it must have been different because I came with a huge trunk with all kinds of things in it," replied Vera.

"We were told we could only bring what we were able to carry, so my brother and I arrived at the station wearing two sets of underwear, two shirts, two pullovers and two coats, and we were also carrying a suitcase full of more clothes," said Steven.

"My mother made a list of what I was to take, but we were allowed to take so little that the list just went out of the window. I brought almost nothing with me, not even a photograph," said Lisa.

"I was more fortunate. I still have two embroidered face towels that I brought in the trunk and lots of other things," said Vera.

"I can remember asking if I could make a dress when I got to England, because I had not even been able to bring an extra dress," Lisa recalled.

"You had a very small case," remarked Vera.

"Exactly as they told us," was the reply. "Tell me, were your parents allowed on the platform to say goodbye, Vera?"

Vera's passport

"No, they stood behind barriers away from the train. Nobody was allowed on the platform. I don't remember the last words my parents said to me. I was on the train and I could see them waving their white handkerchiefs from behind the barriers."

"My brother and I arrived at the railway station looking like scarecrows with our many layers of clothes. At the station, we had to show the Nazis that we could carry all our cases," Steven remembered. "Before we left, my parents told me to be well-behaved."

"Be good wherever you come to. Mind your manners," Lisa said, copying what her mother had told her.

"Yes, 'Remember who you are,'" Steven said, repeating his parents' words. "But it was only when I became a father myself that I realised what they must have gone through, saying goodbye to us. Now I know how difficult it is when you see refugees today who are looking for their families."

"In Nuremberg, they did let our parents onto the platform," Lisa commented. "I had a boyfriend called Lutz and his parents would not let go of his hand. They ran along the platform as the train pulled out, holding on to his hands. My mother let my hand go and stood on the platform. The little children's parents were all running alongside the train, not knowing if they would ever see their children again."

Our lonely journey

"We left the station and I can remember more and more children being squashed in," said Lisa. "The train went right through Germany and stopped several times. Each time, more children got on and we all had to move up. There wasn't any room and as the little ones climbed on with their rag dolls, we all moved up again. At each station, there were all the goodbyes. All the children were wearing big blue and white labels," she said, holding her hands out to demonstrate the size. "Huge labels, like you might put around cattle."

Tears on the journey

"I don't remember the colour of the labels or really very much about leaving on the train," said Vera. "I remember an older boy sitting opposite me, who told me I had been crying a few minutes earlier. Now all I wanted was the window seat. His comment has stayed in my memory ever since."

"When we got to the Czech/German border, my uncle Rudolf boarded the train with his wife, and they stayed with me for the rest of the journey through Germany until we reached Holland. On the Dutch border, my parents had arranged for some family friends to travel on the train to the coast, where we were going to catch the ferry."

"I don't remember much of the journey myself," said Steven, "but I do remember being excited about going to England on a train. I had never been on such a long trip, across the channel. I do remember that when we arrived at the Dutch border, the German customs official came

Arrival in England

11

into our compartment, where there were eight or ten boys. He chose to look at Walter's case, and it was so tightly packed that we could not put everything back afterwards. So on top of everything else, we had underwear and socks hanging out of our coat pockets when we arrived in England."

"It was a difficult journey," reflected Lisa. "There were soldiers on the train too, so we had some strange looks, particularly with our labels on. But I was madly in love with Lutz, so it softened the blow a little bit. I was also kept busy looking after the little ones."

"How old were you then?" asked Steven.

"I was one of the oldest on the train because I was 16 at the time and that was the oldest you could be on the *Kindertransport*. I was fortunate to have Lutz to cling to. I was very upset and it was a long journey. However, there were many children who didn't know anyone, and of course none of us knew the place we were going to."

"All I can really remember is being confused by everything," said Vera. "One minute I was in Prague waving to my parents and before I knew it, I was in a strange country with strange people, just hoping to see my parents soon."

Arrival in England

"I arrived in England on 1 June 1939, but I don't remember anything about the boat trip or our journey into London," said Vera. "The funny thing is, I don't remember anybody being there at Liverpool Street station at all. All I can remember is sitting among a whole group of children. Everyone was being collected and taken somewhere and I thought that nobody was going to come for me. Then a woman arrived from Suffolk and took two other children and me in a car. It was dark as we drove along and I can remember asking her to stop the car because I was travel-sick several times."

The first Kindertransport *arrives in Harwich, England*

"I didn't remember the boat journey either," said Steven, "but I do remember the reception at the station. It was a big culture shock. It was a terribly hot day and they served us a hot cup of tea when we arrived. In Germany, if you were hot you drank a glass of cold water, but a cup of tea? Then they gave us white bread..."

"Oh yes! White bread," said both Vera and Lisa together. "We had never seen that before."

"It was egg sandwiches," continued Steven. "It all got stuck in our throats because we were so thirsty. The women hugged us all the time and we got covered in make-up. But worse was to come. The train from Harwich to Liverpool Street station in London was out of date and very slow. As it came through the East End of London, we saw houses that had lost their roofs or were boarded up. Liverpool Street station must have been magnificent in 1850, but it was now 1939. It was far from wonderful."

"It was very dark and dingy, wasn't it?" said Lisa.

"Yes," replied Steven. "This was supposed to be the Garden of Eden we were coming to and it was a real disappointment."

"When we arrived, it was already the middle of winter," said Lisa. "We had only made it as far as Holland when the war broke out, so 30 or 40 of us were still in Holland. We stayed there several months until we were brought over, even though the war had already started. I remember arriving at Liverpool Street station very quietly in the middle of the night. It must have been the collection point for all the *Kindertransport* children. I just remember standing in the dark station and feeling very, very cold."

"When I arrived at the village where I was to stay for a while, the telephone rang and my parents were on the other end," Vera remembered. "I think I cried so much I could hardly talk to them. I was so homesick, all I wanted to do was go home. But I could not. And of course, I did not know that I would never see my home again."

New families, new friends

"People tried to be good to me here in England, but I was pushed from place to place, from pillar to post really," said Lisa. "I was first put with a lawyer in Wimbledon, where I was treated like a maid. Then I was sent to Sutton Coldfield; and from there I was asked to go to Warwick Castle. An amazing thing had happened. My mother had escaped the Nazis and gone to Switzerland, and had now made it to England. She was also being interviewed in Warwick.

Vera, Mr Faires and Betty

"The British Government were worried about my mother's attitude to Germany. She hated the Nazis, but told them that she still loved her country. As a result, we were both put in special camps. She was sent to the Isle of Man and I was held at Lingfield Racecourse. Eventually I was sent to live in Nottingham. What happened to you when you arrived, Vera?"

"I did not go to quite so many places," she replied. "First I was sent to live for a short while in a vicarage in Suffolk. The vicar was not very nice to me. When I said I hoped that I would like the family I was to be living with next, he told me I was very selfish and I should hope that they would like me. A few weeks later, I went to live with Mr and Mrs Faires and their daughter, Betty.

15

Poor Betty! She had sixpence pocket money and her parents thought it would be good for her to share, so when I arrived we got threepence each. We had little in common, but Betty was a good friend to me. Mr Faires was a very kind man. He was not Jewish, but he understood exactly how I felt and did everything he could for me. I was well treated and sent to the same boarding school as Betty. I certainly didn't have a bad childhood, but it was a very lonely childhood."

"I was put into a completely different situation," said Steven. "I was placed in a hostel run by a Jewish charity in Margate in Kent. There were 60 boys there. My brother was one of the youngest, and the oldest were twin brothers who were 16 years old. They had already been sent to a concentration camp before they left Germany. In the hostel, food was very carefully controlled. We had porridge and two slices of toast for breakfast and 'anti-aircraft soup' for lunch. Anti-aircraft soup had large bones in it which we used to say were like anti-aircraft guns in the soup. On Sundays, we were given fruit cake, which we traded for daily rations of toast with other boys who liked to stockpile the fruit cake.

"As soon as we could say '*pliss*' and '*tank yoo*' we were sent to a local school, where we quickly learned English with the other kids. When you have to speak a foreign language, you learn very quickly."

"Did you know English before you came to England, Lisa?" asked Vera.

"Very little. For example, 'How do you become a bus?', which meant 'How do you catch a bus?" she said, laughing.

Vera with Betty

Waiting to go home

"I always wanted to go back home," said Lisa thoughtfully.

"It never entered my head that we would not. During my whole childhood in England, I was sure we would go back to our families again," replied Vera. "We were just simply waiting."

"But I never intended to go back," said Steven. "I was really lucky. My parents managed to leave Germany less than two days before the war began, and so eventually they came to live near us at the hostel. We had never wanted to go back, but now we did not need to. I started work at 14 as an apprentice toolmaker and then later I joined the Air Training Corps and started to train to be a navigator. When my Station Officer discovered I was German, he would not let me fly, so I decided to join the Home Guard instead. We were classed as 'friendly enemy aliens', which meant we could do most things, but we were not allowed out of the house between eight at night and eight in the morning, unless we were on duty."

Lisa, 1940

"I was conscripted into factory work for the war effort," said Lisa. "I made friends with the factory girls and tried to put Germany out of my mind. But it was difficult because there were many things I was not allowed to do as a German. If I stayed out too late at a dance, I was called to the police station the next day to explain myself. That was what life was like as a German living in England. It seemed strange that we were given refuge here because we were fleeing the Germans, but then we were closely watched because we were German."

Steven and Walter

"My first problem was learning English and then I went to school while I was waiting to go home," said Vera. "At school, they learned that my mother was German, so they decided to play a game pretending that I was a German spy. I felt terrible. There were a couple of children who had run away from boarding school and I felt jealous that they had somewhere to run to. All the time I would imagine that the war would be over and that I could go back to my parents soon. They wrote to me every day while it was still possible – until eventually the letters became less frequent and then stopped.

"One day, one of the other teachers walked into our class and said something to our teacher. She then announced that the war had come to an end. I was so excited I just shouted 'Hurray' at the top of my voice, because now I would be able to go home. I was sent out of the room for creating too much noise. It took me a little while to realise that I would not be going back home. Gradually, I heard that everybody was dead – my parents, my grandmother, my aunts and uncles. There was nobody to go back to. This was terrible."

Vera and Patch

A new life in England

"Once the war was over and it became clear that there was nothing to return to, I got married and tried to make a new life here," said Lisa. "It was not easy as I still wanted to go back to Germany. I think my mother had given me a deep feeling about being German. I felt that once the Nazis had gone, I would be able go back to my culture and country."

"During the war, I had become interested in what was to happen to Jews in the future, and I wanted Jews to have their own country," said Steven. "After the war, I helped to smuggle people into Palestine, before it became Israel. The British Government did not want large numbers of Jews to go there, but there were thousands of refugees who had nowhere else that they could go to. I felt very proud to help them. I felt I was doing something for humanity. When Israel became a country in its own right, I went and joined the army there and for several years I was a soldier. I was pleased to be helping to protect the new state. After that, I began to think about my education and coming back to England."

Lisa, 1942

"I went to Israel too after the war," said Vera. "I went to work on a kibbutz, a farming settlement, for a while. That was where I met Avram, my husband-to-be. Avram had lived in Poland right through the Nazi era and had somehow managed to survive very difficult circumstances, although his family did not.

Steven with classmates in England

19

After working in England after the war, he too had gone to Israel to work on the same kibbutz. We married there and came back to England several years later. I became a teacher and taught immigrant children who were learning English for the first time. So often I knew just exactly how they were feeling in a new country with a new language and new friends.

"But for many years, I don't think I really understood what had been done for me. For a long time, I blamed my parents for sending me to England. I felt they had sent me from a very happy home into a very lonely life.

Vera with Avram

I think they were right to save my life, but as a young girl it was difficult to understand this."

"I felt the same as you, Vera," said Lisa. "I did not appreciate it. I was a little nervous and excited at the time, but as I look back now, I know exactly what I was saved from. Thank goodness for the *Kindertransport*. How I wish it had started earlier and how I wish it had been more than 10,000 children."

The past and the future

"But the funny thing is that if I had to live my life again, I would not change a single part of it," said Steven. "We had lots of problems and difficult experiences, but I think those difficulties have helped to shape my life and make me the person that I am. I feel I have become extremely tolerant, although I really cannot bear to see waste of any kind anywhere. I hope I have passed some of this on to my children. What I would like to know is what one can do today. Thousands of people are suffering because they are of a different religion or nationality. It is very sad. I think if I were younger, I would probably spend time trying to help somehow. I think it's the only thing that one can do as an individual. I always feel I want to do something."

"Maybe because we have had the experience of losing family and all the things that happened to us, we can identify when we see refugee children or families who are suffering. We can feel for them, but we also feel very disappointed that such things are still going on," said Vera.

Lisa nodded in agreement. "After what we and many others have gone through, it's really time we learned to show a bit more care and understanding."

"Maybe we can do something in just a small way, in our own lives to try and help where we can," reflected Vera. "I noticed when I was a teacher how often people would not understand some of the children who had just arrived in this country. I had to explain many times that just because we do things in a certain way, it does not make them right. If children from other cultures do things in a different way, it does not have to mean that they are doing them the wrong way."

21

"It's also important to remember what a country can do if it wants to," commented Steven. "I think the *Kindertransport* was a fantastic achievement. Everything was organised and the first trains started rolling into England only a few weeks after *Kristallnacht*. I am greatly indebted to the people of this country."

"It was indeed a good thing," agreed Vera, "but more could have been done."

"And now the tide is turning. See how few refugees are accepted here," said Steve sternly.

"Very few actually," agreed Lisa.

Vera was shaking her head just a little.

"Really, it's terrible; it's appalling. It could be us out there with nowhere to go... and yet here we are 60 years later."

Maybe this is why remembering the stories of people like Steven, Vera and Lisa is so important. Not just because it is interesting to learn about their experiences, but also because they really could be anyone, anywhere, at any time.